# FAMINE

# FAMINE

CHRISTOPHER LAMPTON

---

THE MILLBROOK PRESS
BROOKFIELD, CONNECTICUT
A DISASTER! BOOK

Cover photo courtesy of the United Nations
(UN photo 164659/John Isaac)

Published by The Millbrook Press
2 Old New Milford Road
Brookfield, Connecticut 06804

Photographs courtesy of: The Bettmann Archive: pp. 6, 9, 22, 34; United Nations: pp. 12 (Gamma), 36, 39 (Witlin); Photo Researchers: pp. 13 (top, © Joseph Nettis, 1981; bottom, © B. Grunzweig), 19 (© Soames Summerhays), 20 (Jean-Loup, Science Photo Library); Wide World Photos: pp. 17, 31, 41; Giraudon/Art Resource, NY: p. 24; Scala/Art Resource, NY: p. 26; UPI/Bettmann: p. 29. Diagram by Pat Scully.

Library of Congress Cataloging-in-Publication Data

Lampton, Christopher.
Famine / by Christopher Lampton.
p.  cm.—(A Disaster! book)
Includes bibliographical references and index.
Summary: This book investigates the causes and effects of famine, gives accounts of famines throughout history and presents ways in which famines can be prevented.
ISBN 1-56294-317-0
1. Famines—Juvenile literature. I. Title. II. Series: Lampton, Christopher. Disaster! book.
HC79.F3L36   1994
363.8—dc20     93-9428  CIP  AC

# CONTENTS

*Many lost their farms during the Irish Potato Famine of 1845–49. In this engraving, an evicted family huddles in a straw hut and despairs.*

# THE IRISH POTATO FAMINE

The time: the fall of 1845. The place: Ireland. The event: one of the great disasters of the nineteenth century.

You are the child of a proud farmer. The farm on which you live isn't very large, less than an acre, and there is only one crop growing on it: potatoes. You and your family eat most of the potatoes that you grow and sell the rest to people in the nearby city. Sometimes it seems like potatoes are the only food that you eat. You'd give anything for a juicy steak or chicken dinner; but you are grateful that you have the potatoes. Without them, you'd starve.

One day, you walk out into the field filled with potatoes to discover something strange and frightening. A funny white growth has appeared on the leaves of the potato plants. You dig up a potato, only to discover that it is small and wrinkled. The potatoes are dying!

You run into the house to tell your father, but he already knows. He sits quietly in front of the window, staring into space. He tells you in a solemn voice about the disease that has begun killing potatoes throughout Ireland. It is called the *potato blight.* It began in America, he has heard, and then it came to Holland, France, and Great Britain. And now it is here, in Ireland, your home.

"What can we do?" you ask. "Nothing," he says. "When the potatoes begin to die, we can only pray that some of them will survive. Because if the potatoes don't survive, neither will we."

But your prayers have little effect on the potato blight. Your family has saved a little money from earlier years and is able to pay the rent throughout the winter. But the next summer the potato blight comes again and all of your potatoes die on the vine. Because your family has no potatoes, your parents must spend their hard-earned money on other foods, which are very expensive. But then they are unable to pay the rent. This forces your family to leave the farm and move into a small apartment in the city, which you share with two other families. It is crowded and uncomfortable, and you immediately miss the farm on which you have spent all of your life.

Your father begins to look for a job in the city, but there is none to be found. All of the jobs have been taken by other farmers who have lost their farms due to the potato blight.

Soon, the family is out of money and is thrown out of the apartment. Your father takes you to a building where many poor people live, but what you see when you enter the building is even more terrifying than the potato blight itself. You are surrounded by starving people, many of them dressed only in rags. Some of them are moaning in pain. Others hold their hands out to you, asking for food. But you have none to give. If you did, you would eat it yourself, because your stomach is so empty that it aches. You can think of

Driven from their farms, some victims of the potato blight found neither new work nor homes. Many people, like those in this engraving, resorted to living in poorhouses where they received minimal food and help.

only the potatoes that you no longer have to eat. You have long ago abandoned dreams of steaks and chickens.

You spend the night standing against a stone wall, unable to sleep, listening to the moans of starving people around you. The next morning, your father goes to his brother and borrows some money. Within hours, you find yourself on a ship crossing the Atlantic Ocean to America, where you will begin a new life, one in which you hope you'll never again experience a *famine.*

# WHAT IS
# A FAMINE?

The Irish Potato Famine is one of the famines best known to Americans, probably because it happened fairly recently and ties in so closely with U.S. history. Many of the 1.5 million people who left Ireland at the height of the famine moved to the United States and have descendants living here today. The reader of this book may well be related to some of those refugees from the notorious potato blight.

A famine happens when there isn't enough food to go around. You may experience your own temporary "famines" when you look into the refrigerator only to find it empty. But a *real* famine takes place when thousands or even millions of people lack sufficient food for weeks, months, or even years on end. And it can't be solved simply by going to the grocery store. In a real famine, even the grocery store doesn't have enough food. In fact, the grocery store may no longer exist.

*Famines happen when thousands and even millions of people lack food for long periods of time. The children in this photo are victims of a famine during the 1970s affecting 30 million people in six West African nations.*

The effect of a famine is to make people too weak to work, play—or live. Millions of people can die in a famine. The economies of entire nations can be paralyzed by famine. And in case you have the idea that the great famine disasters are things of the past, consider that there may be one or more major famines taking place somewhere in the world even as your read this book.

*American consumers at a supermarket checkout: Famines rarely occur in developed nations like the United States where food is readily available.*

*Even so, many in the population cannot afford food and may go hungry, like the man in this photo.*

Those of us who live in the countries of the world known as the *developed nations*—wealthy nations that can meet most of their population's needs, such as the United States—take it for granted that food will be plentiful and always available. If you have the money to buy food, all you have to do is walk into a store and buy it. But there are other parts of the world where this is not so. The food supply in many nations is so unpredictable that even a change in the weather can cut it off. Some parts of Africa have been hit repeatedly by famine in recent decades. And even the developed nations can suffer from famine. The countries that once made up the USSR experienced several famine periods in the course of the twentieth century. Much of Europe has undergone famine in past centuries.

Famine is not only a great disaster in its own right, but it is a part of many other disasters. *Drought* or lack of water, for instance, can cause famine. Ironically, so can floods—as well as earthquakes and plagues of insects. War can bring on famine by cutting off food supplies, as happened in the East African country of Somalia in 1992. Even changes in a country's economy can create a famine by making food so expensive that the average person can no longer afford it. This happened in India in the 1940s, leading to the deaths of 1.5 million people.

In this book, we'll look at the causes of famines, the historical record of famines, and some ways that future famines might be prevented. While you read, you might want to keep a sandwich and a soda by your side. But just remember that not everyone has that luxury.

# CAUSES OF FAMINE

Famine may seem like a simple thing. Food runs out and people begin to starve. But there are many causes of famine. Let's consider a few of them in the paragraphs that follow:

*Drought.* We need water in order to survive. Fortunately, water is a *renewable resource.* When it is used up, it can be replaced. It never runs out. It falls to earth as rain, flows from rivers into oceans. Then it *evaporates,* returning as vapor into the air to become rain again. Along the way, it quenches our thirst and provides nourishment for the plants that become our food. This process is called the *water cycle.* But sometimes this water cycle is interrupted and the water stops flowing. The result is a drought.

When drought occurs, people become thirsty. The crops that they grow also become thirsty and start to die. Without crops,

## The Water Cycle

Earth's water supply comes from, among other things, rain. It returns to the air as vapor. It cools and forms rain clouds, and the process begins again. When the water cycle breaks down, drought—and famine—can occur.

Water Vapor Cools and Forms Rain Clouds

Water Falling As Rain

Water Vapor Rising

there is no source of plant food, which means that animals also start to die. Since plants and animals are the sources of our food, this means that the food supply starts to vanish, and before long famine may be on the way.

A short drought isn't necessarily a disaster. But sometimes the weather patterns in an area can change for years at a time. Farmland can turn into desert. And that's when major famines can happen.

*Flood.* If too little water is bad for us, then too much water must be great, right? Not necessarily, at least not if that water arrives all at once. Floods can destroy crops much more quickly than drought can. Worse, floods are often accompanied by disastrous storms such as hurricanes, which are tremendously destructive in their own right. Not only crops but entire farms can be destroyed.

Even periods of excessive rain can lead to famine by harming crops. When there's too much rain, plants can lie rotting in the fields before they can be harvested—and much of the food supply rots with them.

*The opposite of a drought—but equally as destructive—is a flood. The people in this photo abandoned their farms in Kashmir, India, when a 1992 flood drowned crops and fields.*

*Earthquakes, volcanic eruptions, tidal waves.* You might think that an earthquake or a volcano erupting would be disaster enough all by itself. But these disasters can lead to another disaster: famine. Not only can they destroy crops, but they can destroy the ways in which those crops become food. Before crops can be eaten, somebody has to harvest them, process them, bring them to the store, sell them to a merchant, and, in some cases, get them to people's kitchens. But an earthquake or other disaster can destroy the farm, damage the roads by which the crops reach the store, or cause the store itself to close down. It can even disrupt the electricity that lets people cook the food in their homes. Feeding people is a complicated business, and a disaster can easily disrupt it. The longer it takes for a society to pull back together after such a disaster strikes, the more likely it is that famine will strike as well.

*Epidemics.* Just as physical disasters such as earthquakes can disrupt a society and bring on famine, so can widespread diseases, or *epidemics.* When people are too sick to tend crops or bring food to the stores, famine can join with disease to create a truly terrible death toll. One of the greatest epidemics of all time, the so-called *Black Death* of the fourteenth century, killed a third of the population of Europe through a combination of illness and starvation.

*Even when plenty of food exists, a disaster, like the Hawaiian volcanic eruption shown here, can cause famine. It can make food unavailable to people for days and even weeks.*

*Priests care for the sick and bury the dead in this depiction of the Black Death, also known as the bubonic plague. The plague killed through infection and famine as it disrupted farming in fourteenth-century Europe.*

*Overpopulation.* Famine occurs when there isn't enough food. But what happens if there are too many people? The same thing. *Overpopulation* occurs when there are more people in an area than that area can support. Sometimes there are more people than there is food to feed them. In a sense, *all* famines are caused by overpopulation, if only because the population didn't get smaller when the food supply got smaller.

*Vermin and insects.* Of course, human beings aren't the only animals on this planet that require food. Other animals and insects do too. Fortunately, most of them have their own food supplies that humans don't particularly want to eat. But sometimes these other creatures decide that they want to supplement their diets with some of *our* food. After all, nobody actually told them that our food wasn't theirs as well.

Animals that like to eat human food supplies are known as *vermin.* Rats and mice, for example, are vermin. Many types of insects also indulge themselves in food intended for human beings. Sometimes vermin and insects can eat human food supplies in such huge amounts that it can lead to famine. (Vermin also carry disease, so they can hit people with a disastrous one-two punch.) This has especially been the case during the insect plagues that have struck periodically since ancient times. Insects such as locusts, which swarm together by the millions, can descend on a field where crops are growing and strip it bare within hours!

*War.* Disasters such as earthquakes and volcanic eruptions are disruptive, but no disaster can affect human life and society in such terrible ways as war. Wars have been responsible for famine from ancient times to the present. Wars prevent farmers from planting and harvesting crops. Even when food is plentiful during wartime, the commander of an army or navy may deliberately cut off the food supplies of an enemy country or city in order to weaken its defenders and force it to surrender. The forces that use this strategy of cutting off food are said to be laying *siege* to that country or city. Ironically, there have even been cases where a country has deliberately brought famine upon itself during war in order to deny food supplies to the invading army! When the French emperor Napoléon invaded Russia in the early nineteenth century, for instance, the Russians engaged in a so-called "scorched

*This sketch by German artist Johann Klein shows Napoléon's army retreating from Russia. By destroying their own food supply, the Russians starved the invaders, helping to drive them out. Wars are a major cause of famine.*

earth policy,'' where they burned the crops in their own fields as they retreated. That way, Napoléon's army was forced to bring food in from hundreds of miles away, losing valuable time, energy, and personnel.

*Economic problems.* Food costs money. Some of this money goes to the farmers who produce the food, some of it goes to those who process the food, some of it goes to those who transport the food from place to place, and some goes to those who sell the food. Considering how many people collect money from food, it's amazing that food is as inexpensive as it is.

Even when it costs relatively little, not everyone in a society can afford all of the food that he or she needs. The higher the price of food, the fewer the people who *can* afford it. Not everyone has to be starving in order for a famine to occur. When economic problems strike a country, the price of food can go up or the ability of people to buy that food can go down. Either way, famine can occur even when there is more than enough food for everybody.

*Crop disease.* Like human beings, crops are susceptible to disease. And just as humans can be hit by devastating epidemics of a disease, so can crops. If the food supply of a country depends heavily on a single crop, any disease that affects that crop can result in famine. The most famous case in which this happened was the Irish Potato Famine of 1845 to 1849, which you read about at the beginning of this book. In addition to those who left Ireland, nearly 1.5 million people died. Even today, the population of Ireland has not grown back to the size it had reached before this disaster.

*All of the above.* Few famines have a single cause. Most result from a combination of the causes listed above. For instance, a flood can strike an overpopulated nation having economic problems brought on by war. Many nations remain perpetually on the verge of famine because they are both overpopulated and beset by economic problems. Such nations need only a little push—a brief drought or sudden flood—to send them over the edge into full-scale famine. And once famine begins, it is difficult to bring it to an end.

*Ancient Egypt was the site of the first recorded famine. This ancient Egyptian scene depicts better times: a wealth of fish, game, beef, and bread.*

# FAMOUS FAMINES

The first famine in recorded history happened in 3500 B.C., in ancient Egypt. Although few other famines were recorded during this period, there were probably far more famines in ancient times than now. The reason that so few of them were recorded is that they weren't considered unusual occurrences. Famines were taken for granted as part of life.

The number of later recorded famines is so large, however, that we can't provide a complete list here. Below are some of the more notable famines from the last thousand years:

- *1069*  The Norman invasion brings famine to England.
- *1235*  More than 20,000 people die of starvation in London, England.
- *1333–37*  Famine sweeps China, killing people by the millions. This may have been accompanied by the great epidemic known as the Black Death, which struck Europe shortly after.

*This sixteenth-century painting shows the fertile Chinese countryside. Nearly a half-dozen massive famines have, however, devastated China over the past two thousand years.*

■ *1557*   Rains and cold weather bring devastating famine to Russia.

■ *1630*   The one-two punch of drought, then flood, strikes the Deccan region of India, leading to a famine in which 30,000 people die in a single city.

■ *1650–52* Rains and floods lead to crop failure in Russia. The resulting economic problems prevent people from buying grain imported from outside the country in an attempt to stop the famine. According to one chronicler, some people became so hungry that they "ate sawdust."

■ *1677* Rain once again brings famine to India, this time in the Hyderabad region, where entire villages are wiped out.

■ *1769* Five percent of the population of France is reportedly killed by famine.

■ *1769–70* Drought in Bengal, India, kills between three and ten million people, according to varying reports.

■ *1770* Famine sweeps through Eastern Europe.

■ *1790–92* A famine in India becomes known as the "skull famine" because of the presence of numerous skeletons of the unburied dead.

■ *1837–38* Almost 800,000 people die when drought triggers a famine in India.

■ *1845–49* One of the most famous famines of all time arrives in Ireland as the potato crop is devastated by disease. The potato is the *staple crop*—the chief source of food—of the Irish people, and the failure of the crop brings nothing less than disaster. The Irish Potato Famine is said to be the last great famine in Western Europe.

■ *1868–70* Drought leads to famine and disease in India. One-third of the people in the Rajputana district die; in another region, the drought kills ninety percent of the cattle.

■ *1876–78* Five million people die in India.

■ *1876–79* An especially devastating famine strikes China when a three-year drought settles in on the land. Perhaps as many as 13 million die. Parents are forced to sell their children, and some hungry people turn to *cannibalism*—eating other humans—to survive.

- *1892–94*   Famine kills one million in China.
- *1896–97*   Yet again, five million people die in India.
- *1920–21*   Half a million deaths occur from drought-produced famine in North China.
- *1921–22*   Millions of people die from famine in the Soviet Union.
- *1928–29*   In China the devastating famine of 1876 almost repeats itself. Fortunately, the introduction of the railroad in the early twentieth century allows supplies to reach their destinations in record time, alleviating some of the suffering. Still, millions of people die.
- *1932–34*   Political and economic upheaval in the USSR brings about a famine that kills five million people.
- *1941–44*   World War II disrupts Europe and causes famine in Greece, Poland, and the Soviet Union. The Soviet city of Leningrad is placed under siege by Germany for almost three years, resulting in more than one million deaths from starvation.
- *1943–44*   The cost of rice goes up in India, and 1.5 million poor people die, unable to afford the higher price.
- *1960–61*   Civil war in the Congo in West Africa leads to nutritional deficiencies, which in turn contribute to epidemic diseases.
- *1967–69*   Civil war in Biafra in West Africa leads to the loss of food supplies. One and a half million people die.

*For nearly three years, civil war brought famine and misery to the people of Biafra. The starving Biafrans in this photo await food.*

■ *1968–74*  Drought in central Africa kills five million head of cattle, which causes 500,000 or more people to die of starvation. Ironically, food supplies were on the way from other nations, but did not arrive in time because of poor roads and bad planning.

■ *1973*  Drought in Ethiopia leads to the starvation of 100,000 people.

■ *1974*  Floods sweep across the low-lying country of Bangladesh, India, wiping away crops and food supplies.

■ *1974*  As floods are destroying Bangladesh, drought decimates Somalia.

■ *1975–79*  Political and economic disruption in the Southeast Asian country once known as Cambodia and now called Kampuchea causes one million people to starve to death.

■ *1983–85*  A long-term drought in Africa, which had begun a decade earlier, leads to a prolonged period of starvation and malnutrition in Africa. The drought ended in 1985, but the conditions that make this region susceptible to drought remain. The famines in central Africa are probably far from over.

■ *1992–?*  Civil war and political chaos combine with the long-standing African drought to create a massive famine in Somalia. Water wells and grazing land for animals have always been scarce in this hot, dry East African country. For generations, different groups of people have laid claims to these precious resources and fought one another to control them. In 1991, three of these rival groups joined forces to overthrow the country's president, Mohammad Siad Barre. They succeeded, but then began to fight one another for Siad Barre's power—using not only guns but the country's food supply. Two rival group leaders, Mohammed Farah Aidid and Ali Mahdi Mohammed, used armed soldiers to stop food from reaching each other's people. The results were catastrophic.

*In this photo, Somali gunmen surround a plane with United Nations relief supplies to protect it from rival gunmen. Because of such actions, food failed to reach famine victims.*

31

Soon, nearly one thousand people, many of them young children, were starving to death each day. The situation caused a world uproar when food donated by foreign nations was left sitting at the docks where it arrived, prevented by gunmen from reaching the starving. In December 1992, U.S. troops and troops from other countries entered Somalia on a United Nations mission called Operation Restore Hope to see that food reached people and to help restore order.

# PREVENTING
# FAMINE

In the late eighteenth century, the British economist Thomas Malthus made a frightening prediction. He foresaw terrible famines extending far into the future, gnawing away at the human race. The reason for such famines, he said, was that the human population would keep growing until it ran out of food. Then it would grow smaller from starvation. Then it would grow larger again and run out of food again. This would happen over and over, as long as there were people on this planet.

Yet Malthus was wrong. Yes, there have been terrible famines in the two hundred years since he made that prediction. But there have been nowhere near as many of them as he predicted. In fact, there are large parts of the world where famine is virtually unknown. Why was Malthus mistaken?

Malthus had failed to take two things into account: that human beings would actually become better at producing food, and that

*Thomas Malthus, shown in this engraving, foresaw a grim and endless cycle of population growth and starvation for the human race. Debate over his ideas still continues.*

they would deliberately restrict the sizes of their populations. In other words, it is possible for human beings to deliberately prevent famine from happening.

Even though it is within our power to stop famines from happening, we don't always do so. As the list of historical famines on previous pages proves, there have been times even in the twentieth century when we have failed utterly in preventing wide-scale famine from occurring. In many cases, modern famines such as the one in Somalia have even been *caused* by the acts of human beings, such as wars. Some authorities believe that every major famine of the twentieth century has been either the direct or the indirect result of a war.

One way to stop famines, then, is to stop fighting wars. This is more easily said than done. Recent political developments make it unlikely that a large-scale world war between superpowers will happen anytime in the near future, but those same developments may actually make it more likely that small-scale regional wars will continue to break out. And these wars can restrict the flow of food to those people who are already faced with an uncertain supply.

Nonetheless, there are other ways in which we can make the food supply more stable, so that war cannot so easily disrupt it. Let's look at a few of those on the following pages:

*Modern agricultural methods.* For the past two hundred years, people have become better and better at producing food. The crops that we grow now yield far more usable food per acre of farmland than those grown in earlier centuries. And new types of crops have been bred that are more resistant to disease and the destructive effects of weather. *Insecticides* have been developed that reduce the devastating effects of insects on crops (though these insecticides sometimes have devastating side effects of their

own, such as the destruction of wildlife). Superior methods of growing these crops have also been devised, so that more than one crop can be grown on the same land in the course of a single year. Farm machinery has been invented that greatly speeds up the process of producing a crop, which not only allows more crops to be grown but reduces the chance that something bad will happen to any one crop.

Of course, crops aren't all that there is to agriculture. Animals provide meat, another important part of the human diet (though it is possible for human beings to survive without animal protein). Crops are necessary for animals as well as people, though. (In the United States, ninety-seven percent of all corn grown is used to feed domesticated animals.) When the crops die, the animals also die. In recent years, farmers have learned to domesticate animals that previously were found only in the wild, such as deer and fish. By making these animals into sources of food, many more people can be fed.

Many of the most effective techniques for increasing agricultural output were developed only in the last half century. Unfortunately, it has been difficult to bring these techniques to the parts of the world that need them most, the *developing nations*. These countries, which lack wealth and have difficulty meeting their populations' needs, often also lack the sort of climates and economies that lend themselves to intensive agriculture. Although

*Helping to grow more food to feed more people. A young teenager in the West African country of Benin protects crops with insecticides.*

methods have been developed that can make these areas agriculturally self-sufficient, many of the farmers in these regions are too poor to afford to use them.

*Irrigation.* Drought is one of the greatest causes of famine. The most devastating thing about drought is that it keeps water from getting to crops. Yet a drought-plagued nation may lie right next to another nation that has more than enough water. Why not bring the water to where the drought is?

The human-devised means of channeling water is called *irrigation.* It can be used to spread water around in a more useful pattern than has been provided by nature. One way to irrigate large areas is to build a dam. This captures the water from a fast-flowing river to form a large lake, which can then be used as a source for water to irrigate a large area.

The ocean would also seem like a wonderful source of water. Unfortunately, ocean water contains too much salt to be useful in agriculture. The solution is to run the water through a *desalination* ("desalting") plant before it is used.

*Population control.* If famine is a question of too many people and too little food, then reducing the number of people should be as effective a method of famine control as improving agriculture. And, indeed, the slow growth of populations throughout the developed world is probably one of the reasons that these areas almost never suffer from devastating famines anymore (although there are still isolated pockets of hunger even in wealthy nations such as the United States).

Controlling population size would seem to be a simple matter of telling people to have fewer children. This isn't as easy as it

*Irrigation brings water to rice in these fields on the island of Bali, helping farmers to grow an important staple crop.*

sounds, however. For one thing, effective birth control methods must be available. For another, people must be convinced that they *want* fewer children. In some parts of the world, children are considered to be of economic value, since they can work the fields and tend the crops. But when the crops fail, these same children represent more hungry mouths to feed.

*Climate modification.* Since weather is such an important cause of famines, changing the weather might make it less likely that famines will happen. Although this might sound like something out of a science-fiction story, there are actually ways in which this can be done. Much of the desert region of northern Africa, for instance, is the result of changes made by humans long ago. The ancient Romans chopped down many of the trees in this region, changing what was once rich forest into barren desert. People also contribute to this process, known as *desertification,* by using the same land area for planting or animal grazing for too long a time. By *reforesting* desert areas—growing trees in these areas again—some desert regions can be turned back into areas with climates where humans can live without constant risk of famine.

*Outside assistance.* When, despite all attempts to prevent them, famines happen anyway, it becomes the duty of the rest of the world to provide the people in the famine-stricken region with food. But getting the food where it's needed isn't always possible. If the famine is caused by war, then the routes of transportation may go directly through a battle zone. Or there may simply be no means of transportation available. Worse still, the government of the country may be so corrupt that it doesn't want the food to go through. All of these obstacles were at work in the 1992 famine in Somalia. Again and again during recent famines, corrupt officials have waylaid food supplies for their own uses, often reselling them for high prices and taking the profits.

*Fighting the enemy of famine. Somali children greet a U.S. marine who is part of a multinational force to help feed the starving during Operation Restore Hope.*

In the end, solving the problem of famine may be as much a question of changing the way human beings act and think as it is of finding new and improved ways of producing food and holding down the sizes of populations. While this may sound like a difficult task, it is a necessary one. As long as there are people starving somewhere in the world, those who have food must attempt to get that food to those who do not.

Anything else would not just be disastrous. It would be inhuman.

# GLOSSARY

*Black Death*—an outbreak of disease that killed a third of the population of Europe between 1347 and 1352.

*cannibalism*—the human practice of eating other humans.

*desalination*—the process by which salt is removed from water.

*desertification*—the process by which land turns into desert because of climate change or mismanagement.

*developed nations*—nations that have enough resources, such as food, power, and money, to meet most of their populations' needs.

*developing nations*—nations not yet able to meet their populations' needs.

*drought*—a severe lack of water.

*epidemic*—the large-scale spreading of a disease.

*evaporation*—the process by which a liquid, such as water, turns into a gas, such as water vapor.

43

*famine*—a severe shortage of food.

*insecticide*—a chemical used for killing insects.

*irrigation*—a human-devised means of channeling water to dry places.

*overpopulation*—a situation in which there are more people in an area than that area can support.

*potato blight*—the disease responsible for the Irish Potato Famine.

*reforestation*—the process by which trees and other plants are grown in an area from which they were previously absent.

*renewable resource*—an important substance which, when it runs out, can be replaced.

*siege*—an act of war in which one side attempts to shut off the food supply of the other side.

*staple crop*—the chief source of food in an area.

*vermin*—animals that eat from the human food supply and can potentially spread disease or illness.

*water cycle*—the process by which water falls as rain, is absorbed and used on Earth, turns into a gas, and reenters the air so it can become rain again and repeat the process.

# RECOMMENDED READING

Brown, Walter R., and Norman D. Anderson. *Historical Catastrophes: Famines.* Reading, Mass.: Addison-Wesley, 1976.

Gibb, Christopher. *Food or Famine?* Vero Beach, Fla.: Rourke Enterprises, 1987.

Glaser, Elizabeth. *The Ethiopian Famine.* Illustrated by Brian McGowan. San Diego: Lucent Books, 1990.

Independent Commission on International Humanitarian Issues. *Famine, a Man-Made Disaster?* New York: Vintage, 1985.

Nardo, Don. *The Irish Potato Famine.* Illustrated by Brian McGowan. San Diego: Lucent Books, 1990.

Thomas, Jane. *Population and Food.* New York: Gloucester Press, 1990.

Timberlake, Lloyd. *Famine in Africa.* New York: Gloucester Press, 1986.

# INDEX

# ABOUT THE AUTHOR

Christopher Lampton is a free-lance writer. Born in Brownsville, Texas, he has a Bachelor of Arts degree in radio, TV, and film from the University of Maryland.

Mr. Lampton has more than fifty nonfiction science books to his credit, including such Millbrook Disaster! books as *Drought, Tornado,* and *Nuclear Accident.* He is also the author of nine works of fiction, including several science-fiction novels for Doubleday and Laser books. He lives in Maryland.